Under the Ground

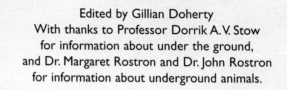

Edited by Gillian Doherty
With thanks to Professor Dorrik A. V. Stow
for information about under the ground,
and Dr. Margaret Rostron and Dr. John Rostron
for information about underground animals.

First published in 2006 by Usborne Publishing Ltd, 83-85 Saffron Hill, London EC1N 8RT, England.
www.usborne.com Copyright © 2006 Usborne Publishing Ltd. The name Usborne and
the devices ♀ ⊕ are Trade Marks of Usborne Publishing Ltd. All rights reserved. No part of
this publication may be reproduced, stored in a retrieval system, or transmitted in any form or by
any means, electronic, mechanical, photocopying, recording or otherwise, without the prior
permission of the publisher. First published in America in 2006. UE. Printed in Dubai.

Under the Ground

Anna Milbourne
Illustrated by Serena Riglietti
Designed by Laura Parker

Have you ever wondered
what's under the ground?

There's a whole world down there
beneath your feet.

If you dug down a little way, you'd find...

...plant roots reaching out
to suck up water
from the soil...

...and hungry creepy-crawlies
munching through them.

Nearby, you might discover
a miniature kingdom...

...where a queen ant has laid
a thousand tiny eggs...

...and lots of little worker ants
are busy bringing food.

A little deeper, a snuffly mole
digs blindly through the soil.

He sniffs a juicy, wriggly worm,
tugs it out and slurps it down.

Running away from a fierce fox,
a rabbit leaps into her burrow...

...where her family is
cuddled up, safe and sound.

If you dug a little further, you'd see hundreds of criss-crossing pipes.

Some bring electricity
to light up all the streetlamps...

...and some bring clean water
to each and every house.

Other pipes carry dirty water away
from toilets, sinks and baths.

Robots crawl through them
to make sure none have sprung a leak.

There's a rumble in a tunnel and a train zoooOOOooms by.

Lots of trains rush around under the bustling streets of the city.

They carry people from
station to station, all day long.

Deeper still, there's solid rock,
patterned with stripes and swirls.

Buried in the rock...

...are the twirly shells of animals that lived long ago....

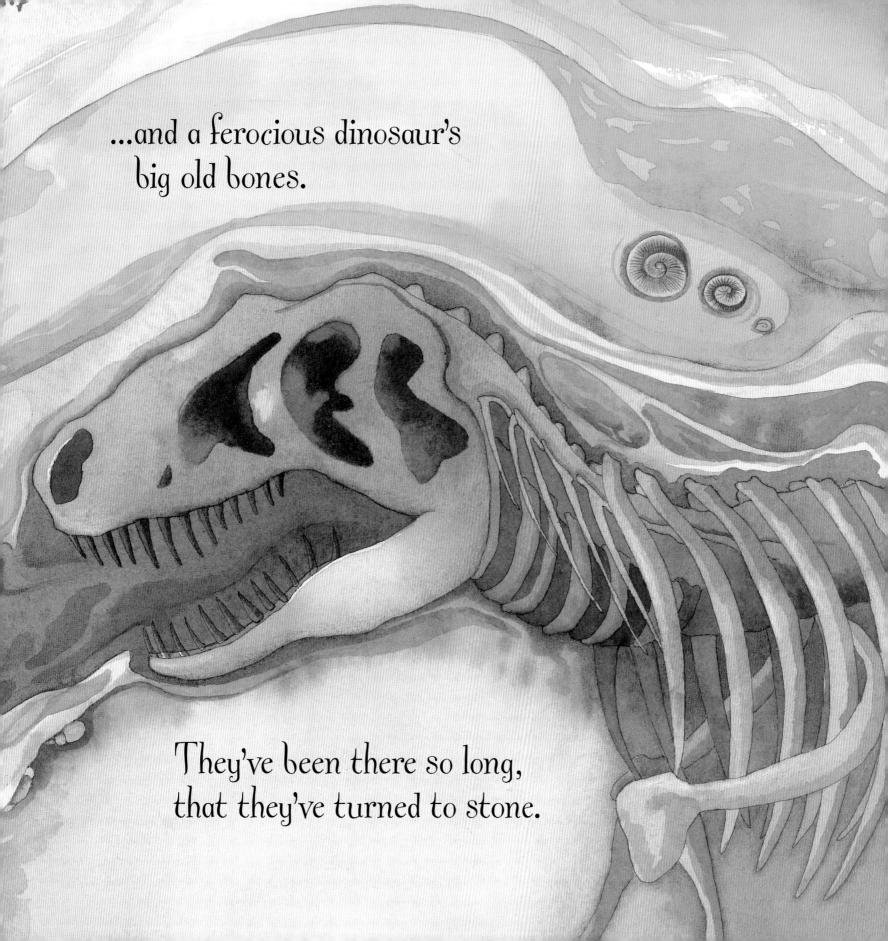

...and a ferocious dinosaur's
big old bones.

They've been there so long,
that they've turned to stone.

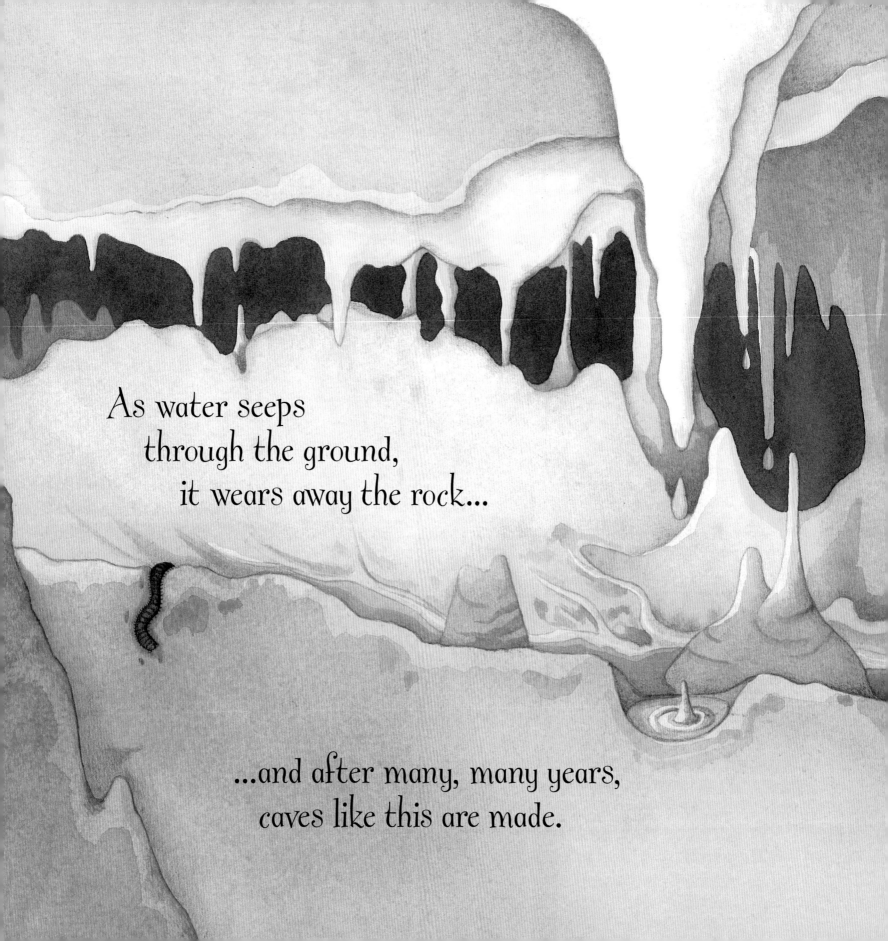

As water seeps
through the ground,
it wears away the rock...

...and after many, many years,
caves like this are made.

In some caves,
there are furry bats
dangling upside down.

Other caves are so deep and dark
that no one's EVER seen them.

Miles underground, twinkling silver
and gold are hidden inside the rock.

Nobody put them there.
They're just part of the Earth.

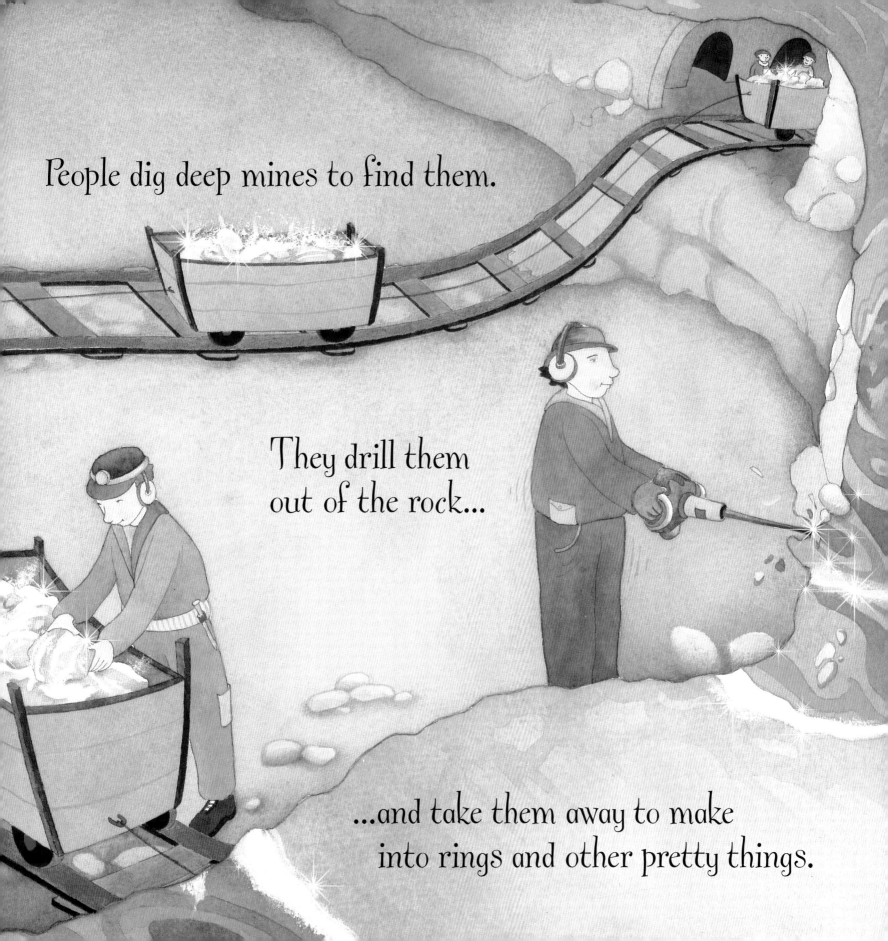

People dig deep mines to find them.

They drill them
out of the rock...

...and take them away to make
into rings and other pretty things.

If you could dig even further underground,
you'd be deeper than anyone's ever been.

It gets hotter and hotter until
the rock melts into red gloop.

You'd melt too,
if you were really there.

The Earth is like an enormous ball.
This is it, chopped in half so you can see.

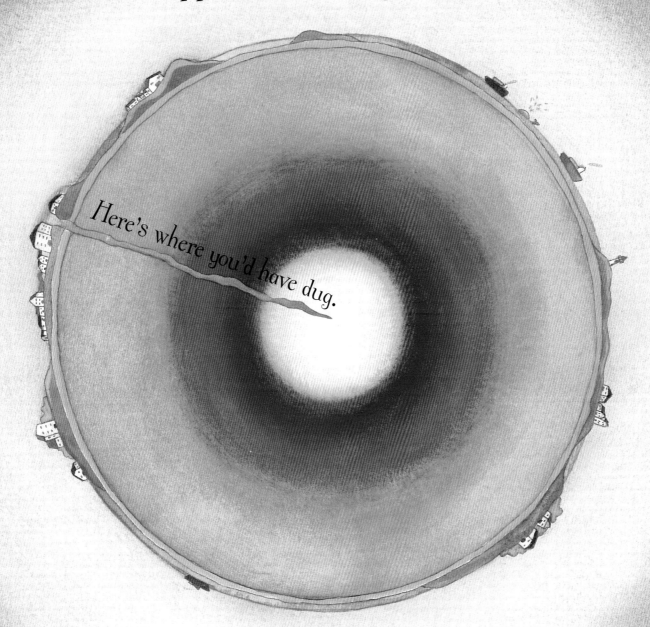

Here's where you'd have dug.

Right in the middle is the hottest part of all.

What do you think you'd find
if you kept on going?

You'd dig, dig, dig,
through stripy rock and bat-filled caves...

...past snuffly moles and tangled roots...

...and after that?

You'd pop out the other side of the world
on someone else's lawn...

...where they were busy wondering
what's under the ground.